First: to my wife Juanita, as usual, she is the dedicated source of encouragement that keeps me writing and does her best to keep my mistakes to a minimum. To my family and my church family who have supported me in my work and encouraged me to continue writing even at this late stage of my life. And to a Christian lady who has been my friend since we were in the third grade, Juanita Bristol McCurdy, who suggested this work.

To those who will take the time and effort to read these words and endeavor to put into action those truths within, it is my sincere prayer that you will be edified and blessed from this contact with the Holy Word of God.

PROLOGUE

The inspired Apostle Paul, in his first letter to Timothy, counseled him in the necessities of being diligent to follow the teachings from God's Holy Word, and admonishing fellow Christians in all areas concerning serving God in His Kingdom. He taught him about being diligent in service of love, faithfulness, prayer, thankfulness, and showed that we should be watchful of how we comport ourselves in order to be an example that will encourage others to become a part of God's family.

Timothy labored with Paul on his second missionary journey. We know from reading Paul's second letter to Timothy that he was taught by his mother, Eunice, and his grandmother, Lois, that he was well taught in the knowledge of the holy word, and was a dedicated Christian. Paul chose Timothy as a co-worker. We see him again in Paul's third missionary journey, and realize Timothy remained a beloved and trusted companion. Paul addressed him as "my own Son in the gospel" and another time as "my dearly beloved son." We can't determine the exact amount of time he was with Paul, but we know he was with him during his first Roman imprisonment; he was with Paul at Ephesus

and was left there to strengthen the church as Paul went on to Macedonia. Paul and Timothy were very close and enjoyed their labor with the church. Paul wrote to Timothy to remind him of the importance of his work with the kingdom of Christ, the church.

Paul's charge and instructions to Timothy were because of two prominent circumstances. The first concern was people being misled by false teachers, Jewish leaders who desired to teach more than the gospel of Christ. "Desiring to be teachers of the law; understanding neither what they say, nor whereof they affirm" (1 Timothy 1:7). The second was to address and set in motion things that needed to be cared for and to correct practices concerning day-to-day administration of the church, setting things in order which were lacking. These are things of great importance in the church today.

Close to seventy years ago, the writer checked and found there were two hundred sixty three different religious denominations in the United States alone. Today there are thousands teaching differing doctrines. Can we think God is happy about this? However, this is not a new thing; it has been happening since the first century. Not to the extent which we see today, but none the less, it had its

beginning a long time ago. We will ponder more on this subject later.

Paul admonished Timothy to "be instant in season, out of season; reprove, rebuke, exhort with all longsuffering and doctrine" (2 Timothy 4:2). Be ready, Timothy, to preach the truth under any and all circumstances because the time will come when people will turn away from the truth (vs. 2 and 3, paraphrased). To repeat: <u>These Things Command and Teach</u>. We will understand the importance of this as we progress.

In this writing, we wish to deal with teaching the gospel in its purity and simplicity, just as it was taught when the Kingdom of Christ was established nearly two thousand years ago. We will address the same truths as were taught at that time. Nothing other than the inspired word of God will be used for points of reason. Discussing God, His Son Jesus, The Holy Spirit, His body the church, His desires for all mankind, there is no reason to give consideration to or accept any teaching other than that which God gave to us for instruction on how we become Christians, God's family. Jesus said: "I am the way, the truth, and the life: no man cometh to the Father but by me" (John 14:6). Peter told the Jewish leaders in Jerusalem: "Neither is there salvation in any other: for there is none other name under heaven given among men, whereby we must be saved" (Acts 4:12). This is stated clearly and is easily understood: we follow the teaching of the Bible and nothing else; it is the only safe and sure way of doing as God intends for us to do. No person has the authority to change, add to, or delete from the teachings furnished to us in order that we should receive forgiveness of sin, be saved in Jesus Christ and be assured of an eternal home in Heaven with God and all the redeemed.

CHAPTER 1

Luke wrote of Jesus: "And it came to pass afterward, that he went throughout every city and village, preaching and showing the glad tiding of the kingdom of God" (Luke 8:1). To use the term glad tidings would indicate that it was to be an announcement of great value and should be received with understanding, joy, happiness, gladness. Realizing this, then we would question, what was it that could be announced which would engender this degree of elation?

Mathew wrote in his gospel: "Behold, a virgin shall be with child; and shall bring forth a son, and they shall call his name Emmanuel, which interpreted is, God with us" (Matthew 1:23). What an amazing projection of a truly incredible event: A virgin giving birth, not the natural and normal way of bringing a child into being, and then to understand that this coming child is actually the one and only Almighty God of Heaven here on earth with ordinary human beings. No, it was not natural; Joseph had been advised that Mary was with a child of the Holy Spirit, and that she would bring forth this son who was to be called Jesus, and that he would save his people from their sins. Read in

Matthew 1: 20 and 21. This would be a fulfillment of the prophesy of Isaiah 7:14: "Therefore the Lord Himself will give you a sign: Behold, the virgin will conceive and bear a Son, and shall call his name Immanuel," and again in Isaiah 9:6: "For unto us a child is born, unto us a Son is given and the government will be upon his shoulder. And His name will be called Wonderful, Counselor, Mighty God, Everlasting Father, Prince of Peace." This was no small undertaking; this was a magnanimous event. Matthew spells out the magnificence and enormity of the purpose of this momentous occurrence. The God of Heaven manifested as his Son was here to "save his people from their sins." Two things are established in this writing: First, if He is here to save from sin, we cannot question that sin does exist, that sin is detrimental to our wellbeing from which we need relief; and secondly, that there is an escape from sin because of His desire to save us from sin.

When God made the decision that He was going to create the universe and all that is in it, He created earth, a perfect world, and there was no sin. He created man and woman, and because of their disobedience they sinned and perfection was shattered. We know from Paul's writing that man was responsible for sin. "Wherefore, as by one man sin entered into the world, and death by sin; so death passed upon all men, for that all have sinned" (Romans 5:12). Paul also wrote: "for the wages of sin is death" (Romans 6:23a). Man is not born sinful, but the inspired word of God tells us that all will sin. "For all have sinned and come short of the glory of God" (Romans 3:23). John wrote: "If we say that we have no sin, we deceive ourselves, and the truth is not in us" (1 John 1:8). "Sin, when it is finished bringeth forth death" (James 1:15b).

So what do we determine in these truths from God's Holy Word? Sin exists, unforgiven sin means condemnation, everyone sins and needs forgiveness, and God sent his Son to make a way for man to be forgiven. "For God so loved the world that He gave His only begotten Son, that whosoever believeth in Him should not perish, but have everlasting life. For God sent not his Son into the world to condemn the world; but that the world through Him might be saved" (John 3:16-17). The rest of Romans 6:23 states: "but the gift of God is eternal life through Jesus Christ our Lord." Paul to the Corinthians: "For He (God) hath made him (Jesus) to be sin for us, who knew no sin; that we might be made the righteousness of God in him" (2 Corinthians 5:21). "Behold the lamb of God, which taketh away the sin of the world" (John 1:29b). The writer of the Hebrew letter: "For then must he (Jesus) often have suffered since the foundation of the world: but now once in the end of the world hath he appeared to put away sin by the sacrifice of himself" (Hebrews 9:26). Jesus said: "For this is my blood of the new testament, which is shed for many for the remission of sins" (Matthew 26:28). "But God commendeth his love toward us, in that while we were yet sinners, Christ died for us. Much more then, being now justified by his blood, we shall be saved from wrath through him" (Romans 5:8-9). Again in Hebrews: "But this man, after he had offered one sacrifice for sins forever, sat down at the right hand of God" (Hebrews 10:12). From these truths we discern certain important facts that should be of concern to each of us. Let's study further.

In the beginning of recorded time, God created a universe, everything that exists, and in this universe He created earth, and on earth He placed mankind. All of God's creation was perfect and to His liking. The human beings that God created failed to heed God's instructions; they sinned and because of their sin, sin was brought into the world. Sin separates man from God, so God made a way for mankind to be reconciled to Him. He sent His Son Jesus to earth to give his life, shed his blood as a sacrifice, and it is in and through that blood that man can be forgiven of sin and reconciled with his Creator. Man took it upon himself to be disobedient and sin, but even then, God did not want man to perish. Peter tells us: "The Lord is not slack concerning his promise, as some count slackness; but is longsuffering toward us, not willing that any should perish but that all should come to repentance" (2 Peter 3:9 NKJV). "Who (God) desires all men to be saved and come to a knowledge of the truth" (1 Timothy 2:4 NKJV). There is no question but that God wills for man to be saved; He made the way possible, but we must do what he requires of us to have salvation. It is our choice, but choose we must. Because there are requirements which we must meet, we will deal with them beginning in the next chapter.

CHAPTER 2

It is evident that the Bible teaches what we need to know about God and Jesus, about sin and forgiveness, which initiates the question: What does all this have to do with my life, and why should there be concern about it?

Let's begin with death. We are all aware of death; we see it every day, and we accept the fact that every person on earth will die. The only exception to this is if we are living when Jesus comes again. Death is certain. Okay, if death is certain, and we know it is, why should that cause concern? People are born, they live until death claims them, and that's that – the end. No, death is not the end, death is just a separation from this earthly life to the next phase of life which is called eternity. James tells us: "Look here, you who say, today or tomorrow we are going to a certain town and will stay there a year. We will do business there and make a profit. How do you know what your life will be like tomorrow? Your life is like a morning fog—it's here a little while, then it's gone" (James 4:13-14 NLT). The Psalmist wrote: "The days of our years are threescore and ten; and if by reason of strength they be fourscore years, yet is their strength labor and sorrow; for it is soon cut off, and we fly away" (Psalm 90:10). "Boast not thyself of tomorrow; for thou knowest not what a day may bring forth" (Proverb 27:1). Simply put, we have no guarantees about our time on earth.

The next question then would be, if death is just a separation, what is the meaning of that? We read of the time Jesus commanded his apostles to preach the gospel; He said those who believe and are baptized will be saved, those who do not believe will be condemned (more on this later). Jesus stated: "Marvel not at this: for the hour is coming, in the which all that are in the graves shall hear his voice, and shall come forth; they that have done good unto the resurrection of life and they that have done evil unto the resurrection of damnation" (John 5:28-29). The Greek word used here for damnation is krisis, which means judgment. Jesus is telling us then from this judgment there will be a separation and a sentence. The faithful will be in eternity with the Lord; the evil will be condemned to an eternity of punishment. Jesus uses the term in his parables, "where there shall be weeping and gnashing of teeth." The writer of the Hebrew letter: "and as it is appointed unto men once to die, but after this the judgment" (Hebrews 9:27). "For it is written, as I live, saith the Lord, every knee shall bow to me, and every tongue shall confess to God. So that every one of us shall give account of himself to God" (Romans 14:11-12). "That at the name of Jesus every knee should bow, of things in heaven and things in earth, and things under the earth: And that every tongue should confess that Jesus Christ is Lord, to the glory of God the Father" (Philippians 2:10:11). These scriptures remove all doubt about death and judgment, the verdict: paradise or punishment.

Again, the words of Jesus: "Verily, verily, I say unto you, He that heareth my word and believeth on him that sent me, hath everlasting life, and shall not come into condemnation, but is passed from death unto life. Verily, Verily I say unto you, the hour is coming and now is, when the dead shall hear the voice of the Son of God: and they that hear shall live" (John 5:24-25). Accepting the salvation for which Jesus gave his life, which we should gratefully accept and live accordingly, is that for which we should be striving. Keep in mind the words of Jesus which he revealed to John in Revelation 21:7-8: "He that overcometh shall inherit all things; and I will be his God, and he shall be my son. But the fearful and unbelieving, and the abominable, and murderers, and whoremongers, and sorcerers, and idolaters, and all liars, shall have their part in the lake which burneth with fire and brimstone: which is the second death."

Contrary to the teachings of some religionists: salvation is not a given, it is not universally given out, it is, however, <u>offered</u> to all the world and will be bestowed upon any and all who choose to do what God has asked of us. Remember, Jesus said: "Not every one that saith unto me, Lord, Lord, shall enter into the kingdom of heaven; but he that doeth the will of my Father which is in heaven" (Matthew 7:21). "And being made perfect he (Jesus) became the author of eternal salvation unto <u>all that obey</u> him" (Hebrews 5:9). *Obey* being the key word here.

It is obvious then that obedience is definitely a requirement we must fulfill if we are to please God. So then it is without question, we must know to what we are obligated to give our obedience. To be certain that we comprehend fully, we must go back to the time when Jesus was giving instructions to the Apostles, the time he knew he would be sacrificed, buried, resurrected, and made preparations for returning to his Father in Heaven. If then it is necessary for us to obey, we must listen to what Jesus intends for us to obey if we are going to be right. It is his word and his word alone that guides us on our pathway. We have need for no other instruction; anything other than God's word is misleading. The Psalmist wrote: "Thy word is a lamp unto my feet and a light unto my path" (Psalm 119:105). Paul wrote to Timothy: "All scripture is given by inspiration of God, and is profitable for doctrine, for reproof, for correction, for instruction in righteousness, that the man of God may be complete, thoroughly equipped for every good work" (2 Timothy 3:16-17 NKJV). *Doctrine*: a belief system, teaching. *Reproof*: correction of mistakes, wrongs. *Correction*: infallible guidance. *Instruction in righteousness*: Teaching holiness, righteous living as God wills us to do. *Complete*: Examples, teaching, and warning that keep us in line with what we need to be in our daily living. God's word is a total and complete package, nothing else needed – no creeds, doctrines or teachings from man. We can only be safe and assured when we heed the Bible teaching.

Meeting with the Apostles after his resurrection, Jesus gave them instructions. "And he said unto them, Go ye into all the world, and preach the gospel to every creature. He that believeth and is baptized shall be saved; but he that believeth not shall be damned" (Mark 16:15-16). This is often referred to today as the great commission. And it indeed was and is great. The Greek word used for gospel means good news, good message, good tidings. It refers to the good news of the Kingdom of God, which was soon to be established, and of salvation through Christ which would be received by those who believed that Jesus is the Son of God and believe in his death, burial, and resurrection. That is the gospel, the good news. The Apostle Paul to the Corinthians: "Moreover, brethren, I declare unto you the gospel which I preached unto you, which also ye received and wherein ye stand; by which also ye are saved, if ye keep in memory what I preached unto you, unless ye have believed in vain. For I delivered unto you first of all that which I also received, how that Christ died for our sins according to the scriptures; And that he was buried, and that he rose again the third day according to the scriptures" (1 Corinthians 14:1-4).

A new era, a new dispensation from God to man was coming. As never before, now man could have the forgiveness of sin. In the old covenant God made with the Jews, there was no forgiveness of sins with their animal sacrifices. "But in those sacrifices there is a remembrance again made of sins every year. For it is not possible that the blood of bulls and of goats should take away sins" (Hebrews 10:3-4). Now with the sacrifice of Jesus, which will usher in the new covenant, there will be forgiveness of sins. "How much more shall the blood of Christ, who through the eternal Spirit offered himself without spot to God, purge your conscience from dead works to serve the living God? And for this cause he is the mediator of the new testament, that by means of death, for the redemption of the transgressions that were under the first testament, they which are called might receive the promise of eternal inheritance" (Hebrews 9:14-15). Good tidings for the faithful Jews. "For this is my blood of the new testament, which is shed for many for the remission of sins" (Matthew 26:28). "In whom (Christ) we have redemption through his blood, even the forgiveness of sins" (Colossians 1:14). "For you know that God paid a ransom to save you from the empty life you inherited from your ancestors. And the ransom He paid was not mere gold or silver. It was the precious blood of Christ, the sinless, spotless Lamb of God" (1 Peter 1:18-19 NLT). "But God commendeth His love toward us, in that, while we were yet sinners, Christ died for us. Much more then, being justified by his blood, we shall be saved from wrath through him. For if, when we were enemies, we were reconciled to God by the death of his Son, much more, being reconciled, we shall be saved by his life" (Romans 5:8-10). "In whom (Christ) we have redemption through his blood, the forgiveness of sins, according to the riches of his grace" (Ephesians 1:7).

It is evident to all then from these few passages of scripture that Christ suffered the brutal death on the cross in order for man to be reconciled to God. Crucifixion was the cruelest means of execution devised by man, and was used by the Romans for the worst of offenders. It required extreme pain for hours before relief came by death. Christ was the awaited Messiah, but the Jews refused to accept him. Their bitterness against him was so great they wanted him dead. They accused him of blasphemy and suborned liars to help convict him with their false testimony. He was brutalized, scourged, beaten, spat upon and mocked, then nailed to a cross to suffer and die for all of mankind to be able to return to God. "In this was manifested the love of God toward us, because that God sent his only begotten Son into the world that we might live through him. Herein is love, not that we loved God, but that he loved us, and sent his Son to be the propitiation for our sins" (1 John 4:9-10).

We have searched these scriptures in order to bring us to this realization. We mortals will live until it is time for our departure from this physical life. That each of us will face death is a given. As we established earlier, death is not an end; it is a separation, and from there, we go to the next phase of life beyond the grave. When we go beyond this veil, we will await judgment to determine whether or not we have been cleansed from sin by the blood of Christ, or if we have remained outside of Christ. Sometime after, when God decides, we will face this judgment to determine our future in eternity: eternal peace, joy, and comfort in the presence of God, Christ and all the saved; or eternal condemnation for those who refused to accept the terms of salvation. It will be one or the other: there is no middle ground, there is no fence sitting, there will be no further opportunities to accept Christ as our Savior. We cannot overemphasize the reality of this nor overemphasize the need to believe in God's way of salvation.

So how do we proceed from this point to safety? We literally have no way of determining the correct answer other than to seek what God requires of us. We must be in agreement with Luke who was the scribe writing the book of Acts when he quoted Peter: "neither is there salvation in any other: for there is none other name under heaven, given among men, whereby we must be saved" (Acts 4:12).

CHAPTER 3

We pointed out in the beginning of this writing that if we choose to seek salvation and be assured that we are proceeding correctly, there would be requirements. Remember, Jesus said that no one could come to the Father except by him. Also, when Jesus instructed his Apostles to go into all the world and preach the gospel, it is evident that believing what was preached was the beginning point. It stands to reason if one does not believe what is taught, there will be no action taken. Also, earlier in this writing we pointed out that there is a danger of false teachers, which is quite evident in view of all the multiplicity of beliefs we witness today. This being so, we must be relentless in searching for truth, accepting nothing other than unquestionable instructions from God's Holy Word, the Bible. Any teaching, any doctrine that differs from the truths of inspiration is not acceptable and will not lead to salvation.

It is truly unfortunate that people follow that which is incorrect and does not provide forgiveness from sin or prepare mankind to be in a covenant relationship with God. As a general rule, people do not know the truth because they haven't taken time to study God's word. Occasionally, some pervert the truth for monetary reasons, but this is likely in the minority. The reality we have to accept is this: if there is no such thing as false teachers and foreign beliefs contrary to truth, God would not have warned about them. It just makes sense, doesn't it? Let's deal with this for just a bit.

Paul writing to the Galatians: "I marvel that ye are so soon removed from him that called you into the grace of Christ, unto another gospel: Which is not another: but there be some that trouble you, and would pervert the gospel of Christ. But though we, or an angel from heaven, preach any other gospel unto you than that which we have preached unto you, let him be accursed" (Galatians 1:6-8). "O foolish Galatians, who hath bewitched you, that ye should not obey the truth, before whose eyes Jesus Christ hath been evidently set forth, crucified among you?" (Galatians 3:1). "But there were false prophets also among the people, even as there shall be false teachers among you, who privily shall bring in damnable heresies, even denying the Lord that bought them, and bring upon themselves swift destruction" (2 Peter 2:1). "Dear friends, do not believe everyone who claims to speak by the Spirit. You must test them to see if the spirit they have comes from God. For there are many false prophets in the world" (1 John 4:1 NLT). "Let him that thinketh he standeth take heed lest he fall" (1 Corinthians 10:12).

Comprehending these passages of scripture, we can readily understand there is a way that is the right and only way. Also, we can understand there are ways that are incorrect. This is true regardless of what man may attempt to teach otherwise. Anyone depending on anything other than God's word will have no hope of salvation. Will we choose God's teachings over what man says? Paul said to the Romans: "Let God be true, but every man a liar" (Romans 3:4a). To the Ephesians: "Let no man deceive you with vain words" (Ephesians 5:6a).

That brings us back to a statement earlier in this writing. There are thousands of denominations in today's world. The Apostle Paul wrote: "Now I beseech you brethren by the name of our Lord Jesus Christ, that ye all speak the same thing, and that there be no divisions among you, but that ye be perfectly joined together in the same mind and in the same judgment" (1 Corinthians 1:10). Jesus prayed: "Neither pray I for these alone, but for them also which shall believe on me through their word; That they all may be one; as thou, Father, art in me, and I in thee, that they also may be one in us; that the world may believe that thou hast sent me. And the glory which thou gavest me I have given them; that they may be one, even as we are one" (John 17:20-22). Can there be any doubt as to what God wants for all believers? Paul told the Ephesians: "And (God) hath put all things under his (Christ) feet, and gave him to be head over all things to the church, which is his body" (Ephesians 1:22-23a). "So we, being many, are one body in Christ and everyone members one of another" (Romans 12:5). "For as the body is one, and hath many members, and all of the members of that one body, being many are one Body, so also is Christ. For by one Spirit are we all baptized into one body, whether we be Jews or Gentiles" (1 Corinthians 12:12-13a). "There is one body, and one Spirit, even as ye are called in one hope of your calling; one Lord, one faith, one baptism, one God and Father of all who is above all, and through all, and in you all" (Ephesians 4:4-6). "Christ is the head of the church; and he is the Savior of the body" (Ephesians 5:23).

All we can read about is one, one, one, one—no place in the Bible can we read of thousands of denominations or a multiplicity of churches. God did not want division, He wanted unity. "Till we all come in the unity of the faith, and of the knowledge of the Son of God" (Ephesians 4:13a). Christ prayed that we all be one, why would we then think it is alright to be divided? We cannot, in all good conscience defend the idea that God is pleased with division. How can we continue to be wrapped in error and feel comfortable in the denominational world?

God's teaching directs us away from those errors in a way that is so easily grasped and followed. The living, all-powerful God who created all that exists and has absolute control over everything wishes explicitly for unity in all people. He has given us a simple blueprint to follow, His word, the Bible. "God hath made the world and all things therein. He giveth to all life and breath, and all things, and hath made of one blood all nations of men for to dwell on all the face of the earth and hath determined the times before appointed, and the bounds of their habitation: in Him we live, and move, and have our being" (Acts 17:24-28a). God is all in all; we need to listen to Him. Why would we not? In so doing, we will lay aside all preconceived ideas that are not in keeping with His will; we can and should put away any and all teaching that cannot be verified in the Bible.

Jesus and the apostles warned of false teachers. They are here. "Therefore, beloved, seeing you know these things before, beware lest you also, being led away with the error of the wicked, fall from your own steadfastness" (2 Peter 3:17). "Beware of false prophets, which come to you in sheep's clothing, but inwardly they are ravening wolves" (Matthew 7:15). "Beware of dogs, beware of evil workers, beware of the concision [circumcision]" (Philippians 3:2).

These passages of scripture have covered sufficiently, and without question, the reason for seeking God's word to answer any questions we might have. Also, it emphasizes and validates the reason that Paul wrote to Timothy and admonished him to be prepared to teach the gospel at all times and under any circumstances. The Apostle would remind his co-worker of the dire urgency in letting people know of the Kingdom, the church in which those who seek salvation in Christ Jesus will be blessed to attain it, and that forgiveness of sin and assurance of dwelling in fellowship with God forever is within reach for all. That which was so momentous in that era is equally urgent today, two thousand years later. Let's explore further and consider the reason for this urgency.

CHAPTER 4

"For He shall save his people from their sins" (Matthew 1:21b). This is the crux of our study. Christ did not die in vain, his leaving the glory of heaven and coming to earth had an exact purpose. It is the greatest event in history and the most magnificent blessing ever put forth to mankind: *For He shall save his people from their sins*. Accepting this salvation and living a life dedicated to Christ means the difference between an eternal life in the heavenly home with God and the saved, or suffering eternal condemnation with those who choose to deny God. We need this constant reminder that we have the choice, but we have to act.

At this point, it would be a good time to refresh our minds about obedience and service. We will go back to the time that the gospel of Christ was preached for the first time to the multitudes and the Kingdom of God on earth, His church, was established.

When the appointed time had come for Christ to return to heaven, He counseled his Apostles. "And, being assembled together with them, commanded them that they should not depart from Jerusalem, but wait for the promise of the Father, which saith he, ye have heard of me" (Acts 1:4). Then he told them: "ye shall receive power after that the Holy Spirit is come upon you: and ye shall be witnesses unto me both in Judaea and in Samaria, and unto the uttermost part of the earth" (Acts 1:8). All things were ready for the gospel to be preached for the first time. It was on the first Pentecost day after Christ's ascension into heaven. Pentecost was likely the most popular feast day for the Jews. "When the day of Pentecost was fully come, they were all with one accord in one place" (Acts 2:1). "And there were dwelling at Jerusalem Jews, devout men out of every nation under heaven" (Acts 2:5). "And suddenly there came a sound from heaven as of a rushing mighty wind, and it filled all the house where they were sitting. And there appeared unto them cloven tongues like as fire, and it sat upon each of them. And they were all filled with the Holy Spirit, and began to speak with other tongues, as the Spirit gave them utterance" (Acts 2:2-4).

In the throng of people, we are told there were at least fifteen nations present and likely more than a dozen dialects. We are not privy to the reason that the people were gathering, perhaps it might have been the sound, but we know they gathered. "When this was noised abroad, the multitude came together to hear what was being said, and were confounded, because that every man heard them speak in his own language. And they were all amazed and marveled, saying one to another, Behold, are not all these which speak Galileans? And how hear we every man in our own tongue, wherein we were born?" (Acts 2:6-8). Some even thought they were "full of new wine."

At this time, Peter stepped forward from the others and shouted to the crowd, hear me my fellow Jews. You are mistaken; these are not drunk as you think. What you are hearing is the fulfillment of a prophesy of Joel (Joel 2:28-32) concerning the coming of a Savior and word of the final dispensation of time: Also, the revelation of God's plan for the redemption of man's sin, the coming kingdom of Christ on earth. That institution wherein the believers could have life eternal in the presence of God in that place that is prepared.

Hear the words of Peter: "Ye men of Israel, hear these words: Jesus of Nazareth, a man approved of God among you by miracles and wonders and signs, which did by him in the midst of you, as ye yourselves know: Him, being delivered by the determinate counsel and foreknowledge of God, ye have taken, and by wicked hands have crucified and slain" (Acts 2:22-23). "This Jesus hath God raised up, whereof we all are witnesses. Therefore being by the right hand of God exalted, and having received of the Father the promise of the Holy Spirit he has shed forth this, which ye now see and hear" (Acts 2:32-33). The Christian era, the revealing of God's plan for man's redemption, the establishment of the church—all came to pass that day.

As Peter spoke to them, he reminded them of prophesies they should remember. The last days had come, and God had poured forth his Spirit to empower the Apostles to teach, and Peter was one of the Apostles who was speaking. He reminded them that they had looked for the coming Messiah and that the Messiah had come, but they had rejected him. He reminded them that Jesus was delivered to the Roman authorities by the Jews to be put to death, but that God had raised him from the dead and taken him back to heaven where he sits on the right hand of God. Peter said: "Therefore let all the house of Israel know assuredly, That God hath made that same Jesus, whom you have crucified, both Lord and Christ. Now when they heard this, they were pricked in their heart, and said unto Peter and the rest of the apostles, Men and brethren what shall we do?" Peter replied: "Repent and be baptized every one of you in the name of Jesus Christ for the remission of sins, and ye shall receive the gift of the Holy Spirit. For the promise is unto you, and to your children, and to all that are afar off, even as many as the Lord our God shall call" (Acts 2:36-39).

The account goes on to tell us that Peter continued his teaching with many other words and his admonition was "to save yourselves from this untoward generation" (vs. 40). Those in the multitude who accepted the message were baptized: Peter said it was for the remission of their sins, as Christ had said. At this time, three thousand people were baptized and the church, the body of Christ, came into existence then and there. From that day nearly two thousand years ago to this very day, what made Christians then makes Christians today.

The account says that three thousand souls were added at that time. They were added to the church, and this is the only way one can become a member of Christ's church, his body. Christ adds those who are being saved to the church; there is no joining, it can't be done. Luke continues: "and they, continuing daily with one accord in the temple, and breaking bread from house to house, did eat their meat with gladness and singleness of heart. Praising

God and having favor with all the people. And the Lord added to the church daily such as should be saved" (Acts 2:46-47). Jesus said: "Ye shall know the truth and the truth shall make you free" (John 8:32). This day three thousand heard and believed the truth, and they were saved by their obedience. As the teaching continued, more became believers and were baptized and added to the church.

This day was indeed a banner day: A day of boundless importance to all mankind. It records the first baptisms of people into Christ, the establishment of Christ's church, that institution of which Christ is the head and of which he will be the Savior. The doors of the final covenant that God would make for man have been flung open, and the invitation that summons mankind to partake goes out to all. Nothing can be more meaningful, more beneficial to all than the salvation that is offered through Jesus Christ. Realizing all these truths, it is evident why the Apostle Paul admonished Timothy to teach and preach the good news of Jesus Christ. THESE THINGS COMMAND AND TEACH. The end result of mankind having lived and being saved hinges on knowing our Savior Jesus Christ.

CHAPTER 5

Let's agree that we are going to accept all the above as truth. Let's agree that it is the most important event of our life to act upon the facts written which have all come from the Bible, the word of God. How do we proceed from this point? What action are we to take? This is pretty much the same question that was posed to Peter on that day of Pentecost about which we studied at length in chapter four. "Men and brethren what shall we do?"

It is obvious then that this is a good starting place to study further. We remember that Jesus, before his ascension into heaven, told the Apostles to remain in Jerusalem until they received power, the promise of the Father, then they would be prepared for the preaching of the gospel on Pentecost. We reviewed the events of that day in chapter four.

We know from what Jesus told the Apostles as he sent them to spread the word. "He that believeth," the result of their teaching, was the beginning of accepting the means of salvation. When Peter stood among the others and preached that day, three thousand people believed what he was saying.

The beginning step in obedience to Christ then is believing. Without belief there will be no moving force, no incentive toward action. The Jews on Pentecost didn't have reason to ask what they should do until they were convinced and convicted by Peter's teaching that they were in error. Once they heard and believed, they needed to know what they should do about their situation. That is what prompted the question, "what shall we do?" They realized that something more was necessary for them to do; they must take action, but they would not have known this until they believed they were in danger because of their error in not believing in Jesus and demanding his death.

The Greek word for believe, *pisteou*, has a much deeper meaning than only recognizing. I see an auto moving down the street. I believe it is an automobile that is in motion; that is recognition. Believing is accepting a concept and holding to it, to place confidence in and be obedient to, to rely on it. The Apostle Paul posed a meaningful question in writing to the Romans. "For everyone who calls on the name of the Lord will be saved. But how can they call on him to save them unless they believe in him? And how can they believe in him if they have never heard about him? And how can they hear about him unless someone tells them?

And how will anyone go and tell them without being sent?" (Romans 10:13-15a NLT). It would not be likely that anyone could or would believe without hearing the good news, the gospel. To hear and believe the gospel will produce faith which will prompt action.

Paul to the Romans: "I am not ashamed of the gospel of Christ: for it is the power of God unto salvation to everyone that believeth; to the Jew first and also to the Greek [Gentile]" (Romans 1:16). "But we are not of them who draw back unto perdition; but of them that believe to the saving of the soul" (Hebrews 10:39). "So then faith cometh by hearing and hearing by the word of God" (Romans 10:17). The Greek word for faith is *pistis* and means firm persuasion, a conviction based on knowledge of spiritual matters. "For we through the Spirit wait for the hope of righteousness by faith" (Galatians 5:5). Believing and having faith moves one toward obedience and action. Without these, we are not inclined to, nor see a reason to know more. "But without faith it is impossible to please Him: for he that cometh to God must believe that he is, and that he is a rewarder of them that diligently seek Him" (Hebrews 11:6).

At this point after studying the above passages of scripture, we can determine that man must believe and have faith if he is to be a beneficiary of the promised salvation to those who believe and obey the teachings of our God.

CHAPTER 6

Believing in God and in Jesus Christ as his Son was the beginning point where the knowledge of and belief in salvation became known. This we have just studied in the history of the Jews on Pentecost becoming believers who recognized their wrongs and made them determined to do whatever was necessary to be forgiven of sin and to be reconciled to God. It was evident from their question "what shall we do?" that they were convinced they were estranged from God and needed forgiveness. In answering the question, Peter told them that they must repent (Acts: 2:38). This being necessary for the believing Jews on that day, it must follow that it is equally necessary today. This being unquestioned, we must study to know more about what repentance means.

The Greek word for repentance is *metenoao*, and means a turning away from, change, change of one's mind or purpose. In the New Testament, it always is used to mean a change for the better. Turn away from sin and turn to God: a 180 degree turnabout.

When Jesus sent the Apostles out to preach: "And they went out, and preached that men should repent" (Mark 6:12). Even before this, after Jesus had withstood the temptations of the devil, it is reported: "From that time Jesus began to preach, and say, repent: for the Kingdom of heaven is at hand" (Matthew 4:17). He (Jesus) told the Galileans: "I tell you, nay: but except ye repent, ye shall all likewise perish" (Luke 13:3). We remember that is what Peter told those people on Pentecost; they must repent. When the Apostle Paul was speaking in Athens having seen that the Athenians were idol worshippers, he told them: "And the times of this ignorance God winked at; but now commendeth all men everywhere to repent" (Acts 17:30). Again the words of Jesus to the Publicans and others: "for I am not come to call the righteous, but sinners to repent" (Matthew 9:13b). Jesus repeated this statement on several occasions, implying the extreme importance of repentance.

Why do we use the term 'extreme importance' when discussing repentance? Each part or act of being obedient to Bible teaching is equally important as all other parts or acts. Leaving out any part of the requirements would nullify the efficacy of the whole. Jesus said: "that repentance and remission of sins should be preached in his name among all nations, beginning at Jerusalem" (Luke

24:47), and that is the exact way it happened as we read earlier in the book of Acts.

Repentance and remission of sins is what God wishes for all mankind. He doesn't wish for anyone to fail and be lost. "For God sent not his Son into the world to condemn the world; but that the world through him might be saved" (John 3:17). Again the words of Peter: "God is not willing that any should perish but that all should come to repentance" (2 Peter 3:9). From the preceding scriptures there cannot possibly be any doubt about what repentance means, and that it is a necessary part of our obedience as we seek salvation.

CHAPTER 7

We are learning about salvation, what it means and how to achieve it. Fully understanding what salvation is and what it means to our future is one of the most important endeavors we will ever undertake. So much hinges on salvation. To be saved is to know that we can dwell forever with God if that is what we wish, but as we pointed out earlier, there are requirements to be met. There are no requirements for not obeying God's wishes; if that is what we choose, we need do nothing. The downside of this would be the assurance that we will not be in heaven with the saved but will suffer condemnation eternally.

It is good that we remember from time to time what eternity means. One word can describe it: it is <u>forever</u>. In eternity, there will be no counting of time because it will be unending. We truly need to ponder this when deciding whether or not we choose to do what God requires. We would do well to meditate on this at length, be certain that we truly understand of the meaning of eternity. Eternity is endless: time without end. In this life, we witness what we call the passing of time; it is measured, days, months, and years, but it comes to an end. It is reasonable that we think on this: we need to know that in heaven with the saved, or in hell with the lost, it is endless. So, let's get back to our thoughts, which we have been studying, about salvation. We recognize that the way to salvation has requirements as we have mentioned. We have covered adequately that the way to salvation is through Jesus Christ. We realize then that the beginning point of achieving salvation is knowing the truth of Jesus and believing him to be the Son of God. Our next consideration was the meaning and necessity of repentance. We have established that the way to salvation would include repentance and after that a confession of our belief.

The Greek word for confession is *homologeo* meaning an admission, an acknowledgement, or a declaration. John declared: "If we confess our sins, he is faithful and just to forgive us our sins, and to cleanse us from all unrighteousness" (1 John 1:9). Jesus made a promise: "whosoever therefore shall confess me before men, him will I confess also before my Father which is in heaven" (Matthew 10:32). This removes all doubt about the necessity of confessing our faith in Jesus as the Son of God; in this, we acknowledge the fact He will be the one who saves us. Jesus prepared for this when he gave his life as a sacrifice to overcome sin.

Paul told the Romans: "That if thou shalt confess with thy mouth the Lord Jesus, and shalt believe in thine heart that God hath raised him from the dead, thou shalt be saved. For with the heart man believeth unto righteousness and with the mouth confession is made unto salvation" (Romans 10:9-10).

Before going further, we need to understand that confession alone does not provide salvation in and of itself any more than faith alone or repentance alone. It is one of the necessary acts as we move toward salvation. The Greek word for 'unto' is *eis*. It is used as to, into, unto, for intent, for purpose, and toward, among others. At this point, salvation has not been bestowed, but we are moving on the path in that direction. So, we are not yet at the point of which we are seeking, that is the time of being saved.

We began this study to discern what salvation means, and how to achieve it. Since we have concluded that we have not yet reached that goal, we of necessity must continue our study and learn what else is required. We have come this far, and we have recognized the necessity of believing Jesus Christ is the Son of God, and that He will be the Savior of all the believers who obey his word.

We know now that repentance is one of the parts of obeying, as is the requirement of confessing what it is that we believe. It must follow then that we seek the next requirement in doing the will of the Savior. That next prerequisite is stated many times in the Bible, and we will consider it next. It is the act of baptism.

CHAPTER 8

Our introduction to baptism in the New Testament comes in the work of John, the son of Zacharias and Elisabeth, who was preaching repentance and the coming Messiah and the coming of the kingdom of heaven. "There was a man sent from God, whose name was John. The same came for a witness, to bear witness of the Light that all men through him might believe" (John 1:6-7). "These things were done in Bethabara beyond Jordan where John was baptizing" (John 1:28). His work was a preparation for the coming of Jesus. The act of baptism was the same but John's baptism was not for salvation under the terms of the new covenant that would soon come.

We also knew of baptism from the words of Christ as he commissioned his Apostles to go into all the world and preach the gospel. His instructions were to baptize those who believed (Mark 16:15-16).

When the Apostles preached in Jerusalem on that Pentecost, they were preaching the gospel of Christ for the first time. There were multitudes gathered there, listening to the message that was taught. Those who believed what they heard asked what they were to do. All of this has been covered in previous chapters. Peter told them to repent and be baptized; this was a necessity for their sins to be remitted. Baptism is the final act of an individual desiring to become a Christian. Unfortunately, there is and has been for many, many years misunderstanding of what baptism means. In order to understand what baptism truly is, we must know what the message of the Apostles commanded.

The Greek word for Baptize is *baptizo*. That word means to immerse, to cover over. To be truly baptized then, one goes into the water, is immersed, and then comes forth from the water. Unfortunately, there has been a great deal of misunderstanding about this act. Many denominations, who claim to use baptism, believe it to mean simply a sprinkling of water, in many cases the pouring of water over the head. This is not baptism; it is not in keeping with the teaching of God's inspired writers and teachers.

In every case of baptism, beginning with those baptized on Pentecost in Jerusalem, the believer went into water and was immersed: this is in the likeness of Christ's death, burial and resurrection. In doing this, one is in fellowship with Christ. Paul in his letter to the Romans made this very clear.

"Know ye not, that so many of us as were baptized into Jesus Christ were baptized into his death? Therefore we are buried with him by baptism into death: that like as Christ was raised up from the dead by the glory of the Father, even so we also should walk in newness of life. For if we have been planted together in the likeness of his death, we shall be also in the likeness of his resurrection" (Romans 6:3-5). To the Galatians he wrote: "For ye are all the children of God by faith in Christ Jesus. For as many of you as have been baptized into Christ have put on Christ" (Galatians 3:26-27). Luke wrote of these converts: "Praising God, and having favor with all the people, and the Lord added to the church daily such as should be saved" (Acts 2:47).

As we are cleansed from sin, we are made one in Jesus Christ and added to His church. "And believers were the more added to the Lord, Multitudes both of men and women" (Acts 5:14). "They that gladly received his word were baptized: and the same day there were <u>added</u> unto them about three thousand souls" (Acts 2:41). "The like figure whereunto even baptism doth also now save us (not the putting away of the filth of the flesh, but answer of a good conscience toward God,) by the resurrection of Jesus Christ" (1 Peter 3:21).

One seeking salvation must believe that baptism is an absolute necessity for one to come into a covenant relationship with Christ our Savior. We realize the necessity of hearing, believing, repenting, and confessing that we believe Christ wants us to be saved, in fact, gave his life in order that it is possible. Baptism is on an equal footing with the other actions mentioned in which we participate in order to receive salvation.

Baptism is a likeness to the death, burial, and resurrection of Jesus. He was nailed to the cross which brought death; he was buried in a tomb from which he arose three days later. As one being baptized, we die to the old person; this is repenting and turning away from the past. Going into the water to be immersed where spiritually the blood of our Savior blots out our sins. When we come from the baptism, we are resurrected, from one who was a sinner to one who is without sin, totally a new person in Christ Jesus. "Buried with him in baptism, wherein also ye are risen with him through the faith of the operation of God, who hath raised him from the dead" (Colossians 2:12). "Knowing this, that our old man is crucified with him, that the body of sin might be destroyed, that henceforth we should not serve sin. For he that is dead is freed from sin" (Romans 6:6-7). Christ adds the baptized person to His body, the church, and a new life begins with a new name: Christian. Paul addressing the Colossian Christians: "Who (God) hath delivered us from the power of darkness and hath translated us into kingdom of his dear Son" (Colossians 1:13). A new name, entrance into the kingdom of Christ, to be one with Him, to participate in the work of Christ, and partake of all the blessings that await the Christian. The ultimate goal, of course, is being in Heaven forever in eternity with those saved. Eternity: it has always been and will always be.

While we contemplate eternity, understanding that it is forever, coupled with the fact that each human will ultimately be assigned their place either in heaven or in eternal suffering, how concerned and how careful should one be? We must search for truth and not be misled with incorrect teaching and gamble on eternity. It is too dangerous to have a misunderstanding about baptism. In truth, we have no choice other than to accept Bible teaching or deny it. If the inspired teachers said baptism is essential and means immersion, how can we deny? Does this not make sense? Will we believe God or man?

If any act is important enough to Christ for him to include it as a tenant to follow, is it reasonable to believe that anyone has the authority to say it isn't important or to change its original meaning? Some denominations teach that baptism is not essential to salvation. Jesus said it is essential. Who do we believe?

The Bible plainly illustrates that the meaning of baptism is immersion, a burial in water; many teach that baptism is sprinkling of water or pouring of water. Which should we believe is correct?

There are other religionists who choose to totally ignore baptism; all one has to do to be saved is believe in Jesus. This is what Jesus said about it: "For I testify unto every man that heareth the words of the prophecy of this book, if any man shall add unto these things, God shall add unto him the plagues that are written in this book: And if any man shall take away from the words of the book of prophecy, God shall take away his part out the book of life, and out of the holy city, and from the things which are written in this book" (Revelation 22:18-19). Are the words of Jesus not enough to cause us to follow his teaching without question? Can we somehow reconcile in our mind that an ordinary human being has more knowledge than

God? God forbid. It is ordinary human beings who take it upon themselves to infer that they know more than our Savior.

There are charlatans who deliberately misuse the scriptures to satisfy their greed, and this is unfortunate. If one thinks this is incorrect, just watch some of the TV or listen to radio evangelists. The infelicitous result is that far too many people are led astray because they do not search for the truth. It is easier just to take someone's word and accept it as truth. *It's right if my preacher says it is; he's a preacher, and he couldn't be wrong. It has to be correct because my mama and daddy say so. It is true because our leader has been spoken to by God in person. Our Bishop tells us we do not need to study the Bible; the church will tell us all we need to know: Just do as we tell you, and all will be well with you.* This is not meant to be harsh or judgmental; it is just the detrimental situation in which many find themselves entangled.

"Beloved, believe not every spirit, but try (test) the spirits whether they are of God: because many false prophets are gone out into the world" (1 John 4:1). "But there were false prophets also among the people, even as there shall be false teachers among you, who privily shall bring in damnable heresies, even deny the Lord that bought them, and bring upon themselves swift destruction" (2 Peter 2:1).

Need we go further? No, we have seen a sufficient amount of scriptures to make us realize what is right and what is wrong. These are not the ideas of a mortal, these are the words of God. We will either believe what the scriptures tell us, or we will believe man-made doctrines which are detrimental to one's soul. We can readily see that baptism is essential for salvation.

CHAPTER 9

As we have seen previously, one who is baptized is baptized into Christ and added to his body, the church (Acts 2:47). One arrives at this point because he has believed the teaching of God. Believers desire salvation in Christ because we accept the truth of either eternity in heaven with the saved or eternal suffering in hell. "Jesus will come in flaming fire taking vengeance on them that know not God, and that obey not the gospel of our Lord Jesus Christ: who shall be punished with everlasting destruction from the presence of the Lord, and from the glory of his power" (2 Thessalonians 1:8-9). Paul said to the Ephesians: "For by grace are you saved through faith; and that not of yourselves; it is the gift of God" (Ephesians 2:8).

We are partakers of God's grace and love through his Son Jesus Christ. The love, grace, and saving of which Paul is speaking are the greatest blessings we will ever receive from God. It provides eternal life in God's presence if we accept it. Paul to Titus wrote: "But after that, the kindness and love of God our Savior toward man appeared. Not by works of righteousness which we have done, but according to his mercy he saved us, by the washing of regeneration, and renewing of the Holy Spirit: which he shed on us abundantly through Jesus Christ our Savior; that being justified by his grace, we should be made heirs according to the hope of eternal life" (Titus 3:3-7). Paul to the Romans: "For if ye live after the flesh, ye shall die; but if ye through the Spirit do mortify the deeds of the body, ye shall live. For as many as are led by the Spirit of God, they are the sons of God. For ye have not received the spirit of bondage again to fear; but ye have received the Spirit of adoption, whereby we cry, Abba, Father. The spirit itself beareth witness with our spirit, that we are the children of God: and if children, then heirs; heirs of God, and joint heirs with Christ; if so be that we suffer with him, that we may be also glorified together" (Romans 8:13-17).

The word mortify, vs.13, is from the Greek *thanatoo,* and means cause to be put to death, kill. Paul is saying to kill or do away with the deeds of the body which will interfere with one's salvation. In baptism, we were washed clean and are free from sin; Paul is saying do not become again entangled in sin. To the Romans, Paul wrote: "Knowing that Christ being raised from the dead dieth no more; death hath no dominion over him. For in that he died, he died unto sin once: but in that he liveth, he liveth unto God. Likewise reckon ye also yourselves to be dead indeed unto sin, but alive unto God through Jesus Christ our Lord. Let not sin therefore reign in your mortal body, that ye should obey it in the lusts thereof" (Romans 6:9-12). Because Christ was raised from the tomb and is in heaven, death has no power over him. We as God's family realize that our hope of eternal life rests with that truth. Again the words of Paul: "But God be thanked, that ye were the servants of sin, but ye have obeyed from the heart that form of doctrine which was delivered you. Being then made free from sin, ye became the servants of righteousness" (Romans 6:17-18). Let's hear this again, "For the wages of sin is death; but the gift of God is eternal life through Jesus Christ your Lord" (Romans 6:23).

Being aware of these truths, do we fully comprehend the significance in that which is now the most important consideration of our life? Think about this and embrace the wonderful truth. Because we believe in Christ as God's son and desire eternal life in the presence of God, Christ, and the Holy Spirit, we have been cleansed of sin and added to Christ's church; we have become the family of God. As His children, we become heirs, joint-heirs with Christ and will inherit everlasting life in the kingdom of God. "Now thanks be unto God, which always causeth us to triumph in Christ" (2 Corinthians 2:14a).

Hear what Jesus said as John recorded: "Jesus answered and said unto him, if a man love me, he will keep my words; and my Father will love him, and we will come unto him, and make our abode with him" (John 14:23). Not only heirs but knowing that God, Jesus and the Holy Spirit will live within us is cause for being overjoyed.

Christians are at the pinnacle of any achievement in life. We can gain nothing higher than the excitement and comfort of being a child of God. "Because of our faith, Christ has brought us into this place of undeserved privilege where we now stand, and we confidently and joyfully look forward to sharing God's glory" (Romans 5:2 NLT). This is the glory of which Paul is writing: "Don't let your hearts be troubled. Trust in God and trust also in me. There is more than enough room in my Father's home. If this were not so, would I have told you that I am going to prepare a place for you? When everything is ready, I will come and get you, so that you will always be with me where I am. And you will know the way to where I am going" (John 14:1-4 NLT).

CHAPTER 10

"There is a way that seemeth right to a man, but its end is the way of death" (Proverbs 14:12): A word of caution from a very wise man. In this writing, we have discussed in depth the basis for the belief of the Christian: how God has made it possible to live forever for those who desire to know the truth about eternal life and choose to do as God has commanded. We have honestly pointed to areas in which religionists are in disagreement with Bible teaching, ways which they believe are right but disagree with the Bible. We only challenge incorrect teaching because of our concern for the souls of our fellow man, and then only with the hope they will reconsider, restudy, and come to a knowledge of the truth. There is absolutely no content in this writing which is not supported totally by the words of God in the Bible. Being totally non-judgmental in writing dictates that we use and follow no other thoughts than those which are indisputably found in God's Holy Word.

Before bringing this writing to an end, we feel it necessary to remind Christians that they will have to be vigilant and constantly on guard to not allow ourselves to become complacent in our beliefs and practices. Living the life of a Christian is a challenging endeavor; as much as it is within our power, we should try to live sin free. We would do well to consider Paul's warning: "Wherefore let him that thinketh he standeth take heed lest he fall" (1 Corinthians 10:12). From experience, we know this can happen; it has happened too often, and if we are not diligent in our activities, we realize that falling away can happen to anybody.

We know that our salvation is offered because of God's love for mankind. "For the Grace of God that bringeth salvation hath appeared to all men" (Titus 2:11). "For by grace are ye saved through faith; and that not of yourselves it is the gift of God" (Ephesians 2:8). "Being justified freely by his grace through the redemption that is in Jesus Christ: whom God hath set forth to be a propitiation through faith in his blood, to declare his righteousness for the remission of sins that are past, through the forbearance of God" (Romans 3:24-25).

What we know from this is that our salvation is not something we have a part in making possible. It is entirely because of God's love and mercy. Man did not have any input into bringing this way of salvation; it is totally outside of human capability. Nonetheless, man has definite responsibilities of which he must be aware, because believing and being baptized is not the end of the story. It is the beginning of a beautiful journey, and it should be embraced with enthusiasm and sincere dedication.

We are rejoicing in the reality that we have found the way, the true way, to a rewarded life in the presence of our Savior. "Rejoice in the Lord always; and again I say rejoice. Let your moderation be known unto all men, The Lord is at hand. Be careful for nothing; but in everything by prayer and supplication with thanksgiving let your requests be known unto God. And the peace of God which passeth all understanding, shall keep your hearts and minds through Jesus Christ" (Philippians 4:4-7). Our joy will be coupled with our desire to abide in the teachings of God's word and to remain steadfast in the service as a Christian.

Let's now give some thought about concerns for Christians fulfilling their responsibilities. "Therefore, my beloved brethren, be ye steadfast, unmovable, always abounding in the work of the Lord, for as much as ye know that your labor is not in vain in the Lord" (1 Corinthians 15:58). Realizing all the blessings and privileges of the Christian, we should stand firmly in our faith and our efforts for the cause of Christ; we will abound in service. Paul's admonition to Titus: "This is a faithful saying, and these things I will that thou affirm constantly, that they which have believed in God might be careful to maintain good works. These things are good and profitable unto men" (Titus 3:8). To Timothy, Paul wrote: "But continue in the things which thou hast learned and hast been assured of, knowing of whom thou hast learned them" (2 Timothy 3:24). "Take heed unto thyself, and unto the doctrine; continue in them; for in doing thou shalt both save thyself and them that hear thee" (1Timothy 4:16). To the Romans, Paul wrote: "I beseech you therefore brethren, by the mercies of God, that ye present your bodies a living sacrifice, holy, acceptable unto God, which is your reasonable service. And be not conformed to the world: but be ye transformed by the renewing of your mind, and that ye may prove what is that good, and acceptable, and perfect, will of God" (Romans 12:1-2).

These truths leave us with no question about our service and responsibilities as God's family. Remaining steady in our faith and, as Paul suggested, that our actions, our life, are a living sacrifice. But God requires nothing of us other than that of which we are capable. He only asks for our reasonable service. Doing what we are capable of doing and shining the light of God's word for others to follow. Remember Jesus said: "Ye are the light of the world. A city that is set on an hill cannot be hid. Neither do men light a candle, and put it under a bushel, but on a candlestick; and it giveth light unto all that are in the house" (Matthew 5: 14-15). We are that city that cannot be hid; we are that candle that shines for all to see. Jesus said: "Let your light so shine before men, that they may see your good works, and glorify your Father which is in heaven" (Matthew 5:16). This is what we are; this is what the world sees. We are responsible for living a life that is an example to others. We will, to the best of our abilities, live our life above reproach.

In our dedication to be what God desires us to be, we will: "hold fast the profession of our faith without wavering; (for he is faithful that promised)" (Hebrews 10:23). Conducting ourselves as we should because we are the family of God will let others see that we are different in many ways. Peter reasoned: "But ye are a chosen generation, a royal priesthood, an holy nation, a peculiar people; that ye should show forth the praises of him who hath called you out of darkness into his marvelous light" (1 Peter 2:9). Christians constitute a holy nation, a monarchy that has Christ as its King. We are a royal priesthood because of our relationship with Christ. We are a chosen generation having been called by the gospel of Christ; called out of darkness into the light of His word. "For ye were sometimes darkness, but now are ye light in the Lord: walk as children of light" Ephesians 2: 8. All of this being true, how could we not be different, standing out in a good way? We have pretty well described the Christian, what he is and should be. Let us now consider the ongoing conduct we strive to exhibit.

CHAPTER 11

When we have been baptized, we come forth a new person; we have been born again, so we must recognize that as babes in Christ we are new, we are beginners and have to learn many things to do as a Christian. "Wherefore laying aside all malice, and guile, and hypocrisies, and envies, and all evil speakings, as newborn babes, desire the sincere milk of the word, that ye may grow thereby" (1 Peter 2:1-2). "That we henceforth be no more children, tossed to and fro, and carried about with every wind of doctrine, by the sleight of men, and cunning craftiness, whereby they lie in wait to deceive" (Ephesians 4:14). As a child, we are totally dependent on our parents. For a time, they must supply our every need. So it is with the new Christian; we are not born full grown, and we are not fully developed. We will need to learn things we should do and things we should not do.

Since we have been cleansed from sin, we do not want to turn again to sin. Paul writing to Titus: "For the grace of God that bringeth salvation hath appeared to all men, teaching us that, denying ungodliness and worldly lusts, we should live soberly, righteously, and godly in this present world"

(Titus 2:11-12). Paul to the Romans, a lesson on grace vs. sin: "What shall we say then? Shall we continue in sin that grace may abound? God forbid. How shall we that are dead to sin, live any longer therein" (Romans 6:1-2). "Be on guard. Stand firm in the faith. Be courageous, be strong" (1 Corinthians 16:13 NLT). "Dearly beloved, I beseech you as strangers and pilgrims; abstain from fleshly lusts, which war against the soul" (1 Peter 2:11).

We have escaped all this as we were reborn, and it is incumbent on the new child of God to refuse to be led back into worldly living. This applies to fully developed Christians equally. "Be sober, be vigilant; because your adversary the devil, as a roaring lion walketh about, seeking whom he may devour" (1 Peter 5:8). Again the words of Peter: "therefore, beloved, seeing ye know these things before, beware lest ye also, being led away with the error of the wicked, fall from your own steadfastness. But grow in grace, and in the knowledge of our Lord and Savior Jesus Christ. To him be glory both now and forever" (2 Peter 3:18).

Satan's greatest victory is when he can separate man from God. Fortunately, we have a promise from God to strengthen our resolve to live righteously and deny sin. "The temptations in your life are no different from what others experience. And God is faithful. He will not allow the temptation to be more than you can stand. When you are tempted, He will show you a way out so that you can endure" (1 Corinthians 10:13 NLT). This is our lifeline, our source of protection. If we are determined to avoid sin, God will see to it that we can.

Before continuing, we will deal with a question that has been posed from time to time by new converts or those young in the faith. Peter's statement in Acts 2:40: "save yourselves from this untoward generation" and Paul's statement in Philippians 2:12: "work out your own salvation with fear and trembling." The question is: what must I do to earn or work out my salvation? How does one accomplish this?

The short answer to that is that we can do nothing on our own to earn salvation. "For by grace are ye saved through faith; and that not of yourselves it is the gift of God" (Ephesians 2:8). Grace is not something we can earn; it is a gift, so being saved is something that God wanted for mankind because of His love for His creation. "Herein is love, not that we loved God, but that he loved us, and sent his Son to be the propitiation for our sins" (1 John

4:10). In this, we see that Jesus paid the price for our reconciliation to God. To the Romans, Paul wrote: "Being justified freely by His grace through the redemption that is in Christ Jesus" (Romans 3:24). To work out one's salvation requires only that we do those things in which God has promised salvation. It is to respect God and do as He has asked us to do in fear and trembling. The only fear we would feel is how great the reward is and to know there is the possibility of failure. This should answer any question about earning salvation; we don't. It is God's free gift made possible by the sacrifice of Jesus on the cross.

We now know many things which we might not have known without this writing. We know there is a God; we believe this. We believe that Jesus is His Son. We have read about Jesus being a sacrifice for sin, and that it is through him that we can be saved from sin and have life everlasting in God's heaven. We have learned what the church is and what it isn't. We know that it is the earthly kingdom of Christ; those in this kingdom, Christ's church, are the saved individuals who by their obedience have been added to that kingdom. We know that Jesus is the head of the church and will be the Savior of that kingdom when the end time comes (Ephesians 5:23). "That in the dispensation of the fullness of times he might gather together in one all things in Christ, both which are in heaven, and which are on earth; even in him" (Ephesians 1:10).

Having believed all of our study about Christ and salvation, let's say we have done what is required to become a Christian. We believed; we desired a new life in Christ so we repented and turned away from our past life. We acknowledged our belief in Christ by confessing that belief and then were cleansed by the blood of Christ as we were baptized, and we were filled with joy knowing that we are a new creature, simply called a Christian. We have done all this, so now we just wait until Christ comes again to take us to heaven. Wait, can this be correct?

As a child of God, is there nothing else which is essential for us to participate in as members of His church? That's a good question, and the answer is that there is much to do. Paul said to the Corinthians: "We then, as workers together with him (Christ) beseech you also that ye receive not the grace of God in vain" (2 Corinthians 6:1). That grace expressed is in the death of Jesus on the cross, the sacrifice that made our salvation a reality. To receive it in vain would be to harbor this truth within ourselves and not share it. Jesus said: "For unto whomsoever much is given, of him shall be much required: and to whom men have committed much, of him they will ask the more" (Luke 12:48b). We have been given much in that we have come to the Father through Jesus Christ. We, in turn, then can do much. The disciples asked of Jesus: "Then said they unto him, what shall we do, that we might work the works of God?" (John 6:28). Later Jesus said: "I must work the works of Him that sent me, while it is day: the night cometh when no man can work" (John 9:4). There was no question; our Lord knew there were things that had to be accomplished. "Then Jesus said unto his disciples, if any man will come after me, let him deny himself, and take up his cross and follow me" (Matthew 16:24). "He that taketh not his cross, and followeth after, is not worthy of me" (Matthew 10:38). The Greek words translated *deny* means to literally disown, to deny utterly. Simply put, that means that we will put Jesus ahead of anything else in our life, that what he asks of us we will do. As we mentioned earlier: "ye know that your labor is not in vain in the Lord" (1 Corinthians 15:58).

God's children recognize the wonderful blessings they have received, being a part of God's favored, His family. So then realizing this, one should choose first of all to worship God. "But the hour cometh and now is, when the true worshippers shall worship the Father in spirit and in truth: for the Father seeketh such to worship him. God is a Spirit: and they that worship him must worship him in spirit and in truth" (John 4:23-24). God is not flesh and blood as we human beings are; we cannot see him with our eyes. Our worship must come from the heart in all seriousness and in keeping with the word of God. Under the Law of Moses, the worship was mechanical and formal but not so now. It is with truth from our heart, and in so doing, we will be led to an ongoing closer relationship with our heavenly Father. To accomplish this, we must know and understand all Bible teaching that will bring us to worship to glorify and magnify our Father in heaven. We can only do this by making a serious study of His word, the Bible. Now, let's go further with our consideration of Christian activity.

Paul admonished Timothy: "Study to show thyself approved unto God, a workman that needeth not to be ashamed, rightly dividing the word of truth" (2 Timothy 2:15). The Psalmist of old prayed: "O that my ways were directed to keep thy statutes! Then shall I not be ashamed, when I have respect unto all thy commandments" (Psalm 119:5-

6). We study the word in order to thoroughly understand and obey; it is the way the Christian shows himself to be approved of God. Studying the word and knowing what is required is the way we know we are correct; there will be no cause for shame. Also, we will not be mistaken in our understanding. Rightly dividing the word means handling it the proper way and understanding what it means, thereby eliminating any confusion.

The writer of the Hebrew letter pointed out that God spoke to people in different ways at different times. He used the term "diverse" and continued by saying that in these present times spoke to us through his Son, Jesus. His teaching in the new covenant would not be as he taught under the Mosaic dispensation. That is why we need to study to be certain we are correct. To the Roman Christians, Paul wrote: "For I am not ashamed of the gospel of Christ: for it is the power of God unto salvation to every one that believeth; to the Jew first and to the Greek" (Romans 1:16). This is another reason we must be certain of what we believe and teach: for our own safety and for those with whom we will be teaching the way to salvation. This will be one of the responsibilities we take upon ourselves when we become Christians; that is to teach others. "Let the word of Christ dwell in you richly in all wisdom; teaching and admonishing one another in psalms and hymns and spiritual songs, singing with grace in your hearts to the Lord" (Colossians 3:16). Paul to Timothy: "Thou therefore, my son, be strong in the grace that is in Christ Jesus. And the things that thou hast heard of me among many witnesses, the same commit thou to faithful men, who shall be able to teach others also" (2 Timothy 2:1-2). Jesus told Saul of Tarsus (later the Apostle Paul) He was going to send him to the Gentiles: "To open their eyes, and to turn them from darkness to light, and from the power of Satan unto God, that they may receive forgiveness of sins, and inheritance among them which are sanctified by faith that is in me" (Acts 26:17). Paul said: "Whereof I am made a minister, according to the dispensation of God which is given to me for you, to fulfill the word of God" (Colossians 1:25). "Finally, brethren, pray for us, that the word of the Lord may have free course, and be glorified, even as it is with you" (2 Thessalonians 3:1). It is the word of God that brings man to salvation. Paul knew the importance of it and emphasized to others the power of the word; the word that needed to be preached by believers. The need today is just as urgent as then.

CHAPTER 12

Let's now give thought to the ways we show that which we profess. Someone once said that "A hypocrite is one who does not intend to be what he pretends to be" (anon). We certainly do not wish to appear as such, but more importantly, we do not dare to be such. One measuring stick that will determine the strength of one's faith is observing attendance at Bible study and worship services.

The writer of the Hebrew letter wrote: "Let us draw near with a true heart in full assurance of faith, having our hearts sprinkled from an evil conscience, and our bodies washed with pure water. Let us hold fast the profession of our faith without wavering: (for he is faithful that promised.) And let us consider one another to provoke unto love and to good works: not forsaking the assembling of ourselves together, as the manner of some is; but exhorting one another: and so much the more, as ye see the day approaching" (Hebrews 10:22-25). The admonition here is not to lose sight of what is of the greatest importance: gathering with our Christian family to worship God. Solidifying our relationship with God to be prepared for what is ahead.

We are not for certain whether the writer was talking of the coming day of judgment or referring to the destruction of Jerusalem that was imminent in a few years. However intended, it does not diminish the importance of heeding the admonition now. We know that at some point we will stand for judgment for what our lives have been or haven't been. We have already touched on the words of John earlier in the writing concerning the need for worship (John 4:23-24). Our Father who has blessed us in innumerable ways expects our worship. True worship is assembling ourselves with our brothers and sisters and honoring God with our thanksgiving by praising Him for what He is and what He does for mankind. We need to glorify His name in our singing and in our prayers. Hear the Psalmist: "It is a good thing to give thanks unto the Lord, and to sing praises unto thy name, O most high" (Psalm 92:1). "I will praise thee O Lord, among the people; and I will sing praises unto thee among the nations" (Psalm 108:3). From the Hebrew letter: "Saying, I will declare thy name unto my brethren, in the midst of the church will I sing praise unto thee" (Hebrews 2:12). "What is it then? I will pray with the spirit, and I will pray with the understanding also: I will sing with the spirit, and I will sing with the understanding also" (1 Corinthians 14:15). In these ways of honoring God, we must resolve to always be faithful to participate.

Unfortunately, not all see this as a matter of grave consequence. We mentioned earlier about putting Christ first in our lives, which we should do. However, it seems that we are not prone to follow this too well. Looking at most congregations of the Lord's church, we see often that our brothers and sisters are not overly diligent about Bible study and the worship service. Our faith and our love for God is measured by how we give of ourselves and our time to honor God. He has given us all; surely we can plan to devote more than an hour or two each week to Him. We sing "O How I Love Jesus," but often by our actions, we do not evince this. This is not something which we should feel obligated to do; it is that which our faith *insists* we do. If we do not participate in Bible study and worship, we will not grow in Christ.

Now we will consider another part of our worship. In the books of Matthew, Mark, and Luke we read of the evening of Christ's betrayal. It was the eve of the Passover when Christ met with the twelve Apostles and partook with them of the feast of the unleavened bread. Matthew tells us: "And as they were eating, Jesus took bread, and blessed it, and broke it, and gave it to the disciples, and said, Take, eat; this is my body. And he took the cup, and gave thanks, and gave it to them, saying, Drink ye all of it; for this is my blood of the new testament, which is shed for many for the remission of sins" (Matthew 26:26-28). "This is my body which is given for you: this do in remembrance of me" (Luke 22:19). Paul explained to the Corinthians: "For I have received of the Lord that which also I delivered unto you, That the Lord Jesus the same night in which he was betrayed took bread: and when he had given thanks he brake it, and said, Take, eat: this is my body, which is broken for you: this do in remembrance of me. After the same manner also he took the cup, when he had supped, saying, this cup is the new testament in my blood: this do ye, as oft as ye drink it, in remembrance of me. For as often as ye eat this bread, and drink this cup, ye do show the Lord's death till he come" (1 Corinthians 11:23-26).

When the Apostle Paul was in Troas, he gives us the time this communion service is to be celebrated. "And upon the first day of the week when the disciples came together to break bread" (Acts 20:7a). He was guided by the Holy Spirit in this, so this is our example to follow. They met on the first day of the week to worship, and this holy time of communion is for remembering the sacrifice that Christ made for all mankind. He suffered the brutal death on the cross, shedding his blood, so we can be cleansed from sin. If we miss the morning worship, then we also miss remembering and being thankful that Jesus died for us. "I speak to wise men; judge ye what I say. The cup of blessing which we bless, is it not the communion of the blood of Christ? The bread which we break, is it not the communion of the body of Christ?"

Paul had a warning message concerning the communion. "Wherefore whosoever shall eat this bread, and drink this cup of the Lord, unworthily, shall be guilty of the body and blood of the Lord. But let a man examine himself, and so let him eat of that bread, and drink of that cup. For he that eateth and drinketh unworthily, eateth and drinketh damnation to himself, not discerning the Lord's body" (1 Corinthians 11:27-29). We cannot put too much emphasis on partaking of this part of our worship; we must be fully attuned to Christ's sacrifice for us as we do this.

CHAPTER 13

In Paul's first letter to the Thessalonians, he advised: "Pray without ceasing" (1 Thessalonians 5:17). It is not likely that we can pray twenty-four hours a day every day, but we can be in a prayerful attitude always. We cannot over-stress the value of prayer for the Christian. To the Corinthians, he said: "I will pray with the spirit, and I will pray with the understanding also: I will sing with the spirit, and I will sing with the understanding" (1 Corinthians 14:15). The Christian in worship will pray and sing in such a way as all who hear can understand what is being tendered toward God and be edified by this part of the worship service.

When we are in our private prayers, as we talk to God about our thanksgiving, about our privileges, all our blessings and our concerns, we are in a one-on-one relationship with the creator of all that exists: God, who is the source of everything we have in this life. We pray knowing that God wants this interrelationship with members of His family. He knows what we will pray before we even utter our thoughts. "Likewise the Spirit also helpeth our infirmities: for we know not what we should pray for as we ought: but the Spirit itself maketh intercession for us with groanings which cannot be uttered" (Romans 8:26). We not only do this for ourselves, but we are instructed to pray for others: "I exhort therefore, that, first of all, supplications, and prayers, intercessions, and giving of thanks, be made for all men" (1 Timothy 2:1). Our prayers are to benefit others; Paul said in so doing "we can lead a quiet and peaceable life in all godliness and honesty" (vs. 2). "For the eyes of the Lord are over the righteous and his ears are open unto their prayers: but the face of the Lord is against them that do evil" (1 Peter 3:12).

We likely do not fully comprehend the power we have when we pray; after all, we are in communion with God. James said: "is any among you afflicted? let him pray. Is any merry? Let him sing psalms. Is any sick among you? Let him call for the Elders of the church; and let them pray over him, anointing him with oil in the name of the Lord. And the prayer of faith shall save the sick, and the Lord shall raise him up; and if he have committed sins, they shall be forgiven him. Confess your faults one to another, and pray one for another, that ye may be healed. The effectual fervent prayer of a righteous man availeth much," (James 5:13-16).

We'll give consideration to one more subject and say that we have written what was intended at the outset. Something that has always been required by God for his followers is to honor that relationship with a return of a portion of that with which God has blessed us. Under the old law, tithing was a requirement. We will not delve too deeply into that as it no longer is applicable. In short, the Levites were to receive "all the tenth in Israel" (Numbers 18:21, 24). There were exceptions and differences to this, but this is sufficient for now.

We are instructed: "Now concerning the collection for the saints, as I have given order to the churches of Galatia, even so do ye. Upon the first day of the week let every one of you lay by him in store, as God hath prospered him, that there be no gatherings when I come," Paul to the Corinthians, chapter sixteen, verses 1 and 2. This was for a specific purpose, but again it was by direction of the Holy Spirit, so this is what is required of Christians today.

Also Paul said: "Every man according as he purposeth in his heart, so let him give; not grudgingly, or of necessity: for God loveth a cheerful giver" (2 Corinthians 9:7). "But this I say, he which soweth sparingly shall reap sparingly; and he which soweth bountifully shall reap bountifully" (2 Corinthians 9:6). Jesus said: "Give, and it shall be given unto you; good measure, pressed down, and shaken together, and running over, shall men give into your bosom. For with the same measure that ye mete, withal it shall be measured to you" (Luke 6:38). What you determine to give back to God is entirely at your discretion. He did not set a specified requirement other than to give as you have been prospered and as you purpose. The Elders and/or leaders of a congregation can only work with what the members allow to be done by the contributions. Local charities, outreach programs, missionary work, etc. all depend on the generosity of the church members. Equally important is the fact that God knows how He has blessed us; He sees how honest we are about giving with a cheerful heart. We all need to think seriously and pray about this.

CHAPTER 14

At the outset of this writing, it was entitled *These Things Command and Teach* and a sub-title was added, *What Jesus Wants You to Know*. Paul in his letter to Timothy told him that he needed to command and teach the things people needed to hear: the things that Jesus wanted them to know, to realize that sin in their lives would condemn them to an eternity of pain and suffering, to know and understand that Jesus gave his life as a sacrifice to defeat sin, and that sin could be overcome by believing in and obeying him, to be aware that those who believed and were baptized into him could have eternal joy in the presence of our Father in that place which has been prepared for the saved.

Heaven is a real place, as is Hell. All mankind, since the time God created everything we see and know until the earth shall be destroyed, will be assigned either to Heaven or Hell when the time of judgment comes. Whether or not we believe this doesn't change truth; Heaven and Hell are real, and everybody will be in one place or the other. There is no middle ground; there are no alternatives. This is fact, not the imaginings of radical thinking to scare people. It is God's promise and

His determination to reward or punish. God's desire is that all mankind would heed His word and be a partaker of the love He has shown for man. Punishment is not what He wants, but it is up to us to determine the result. He has shown us the way, and knowing what Jesus wants us to know is the most important message we will ever receive.

Stop for just a moment and think about this; it is just that important. In Him there is forgiveness of sin and the assurance of eternal life in God's heavenly home. In Him there is joy, tranquility and lasting peace while we are here on earth. In the kingdom of Christ, His church, we can receive salvation; we can worship, honor and magnify the name of God and experience a life that can be found in no other place. We have the safety and comfort of a personal relationship with God, Christ, and the Holy Spirit and peace of mind knowing what lies ahead for the child of God. The writer of the Hebrew letter said: "Wherefore we receiving a kingdom which cannot be moved, let us have grace whereby we may serve God acceptably with reverence and godly fear: For our God is a consuming fire" (Hebrews 12:28-29). One more time, a repetition of the words of Jesus: "Marvel not at this: for the hour is coming, in the which all that are in the graves shall hear His voice, and shall come forth; they that have done good, unto the resurrection of life; and they that have done evil, to the resurrection of damnation" (John 5:28-29). These are the things that Jesus wants you to know. Will you heed them?

The reader will notice that at times scriptures have been repeated, this is by design to emphasize a point; it is not a mistake that some will be seen more than once. The intent of this writing is simple, hoping the reader will have a greater understanding of the needs of man: to realize the necessity of obeying the words of our God. He has given us a Bible written by those inspired and directed by the Holy Spirit; the instructions therein will guide us to salvation in Christ and instruct us in how we are to serve God. The only requirement is that we heed them and act.